The Background of Jewish Apocalyptic

by

W. G. LAMBERT

Professor of Assyriology
in the University of Birmingham

The Ethel M. Wood Lecture
delivered before the University of London
on 22 February 1977

UNIVERSITY OF LONDON
THE ATHLONE PRESS
1978

Published by
THE ATHLONE PRESS
UNIVERSITY OF LONDON
at 4 Gower Street, London WC1

Distributed by Tiptree Book Services Ltd
Tiptree, Essex

U.S.A. and Canada
Humanities Press Inc
New Jersey

BS
1555.2
.L55
1977

© *The University of London* 1978

ISBN 0 485 14321 6
ISSN 0425-4171

208
T67
1286

Printed in Great Britain by
WESTERN PRINTING SERVICES LTD
BRISTOL

THE BACKGROUND OF JEWISH APOCALYPTIC

Definitions are notoriously difficult to formulate, and 'Apocalyptic' is no exception to this rule. A simple definition would be inadequate, and a more serious attempt would not be complete within the hour. Instead examples will be given, in the anticipation that anyone attending an Ethel M. Wood lecture will know something of them. Daniel is the one book in the Old Testament to which the term apocalyptic can be applied without fear of contradiction because of its visions and revelations concerning Jewish and world history. But many scholars also apply the term to portions of other books: Joel ch. 3, Isaiah chs. 24–27, parts of Ezekiel and Zechariah, to name some obvious examples. In the New Testament the last book as commonly arranged, the Revelation (Greek: *Apokalupsis*) of John, proclaims by its title its apocalyptic character, but many scholars would also so describe the Olivet Prophecy in the synoptic gospels. Outside the canon there are many more books wholly or partly of this kind, for example of Jewish writings there are the Book of Enoch, the Slavonic Enoch, the Testaments of the Twelve Patriarchs, two works under Baruch's name, 4 Ezra, and so on. Our subject tonight being Jewish apocalyptic, only Daniel and these extra-canonical works are of concern and attention will largely be restricted to Daniel because it is the best known example, though what is said will have relevance to parts of the other works too.

The period covered by these books is from the second century B.C. to the second century A.D., and Daniel, which in its present form dates from the second quarter of the second century B.C., is one of the earliest, if not the earliest. Its immediate background was the struggle of the Jews under Judas Maccabaeus against the Seleucid king Antiochus IV, who wanted to paganize the Palestinian Jewish community with its centre in Jerusalem. The book is commonly divided into two halves, chs. 1–6 consisting of narratives about Daniel and his friends in the Neo-Babylonian and Persian courts, and chs. 7–12, which are devoted to visions and revelations. However, the first half also has its share of visions and revelations so that the present speaker agrees with those who take the book in its present form as a unity, although some parts are written in Hebrew and others in Aramaic.

The historical setting explains the final form and purpose of the book very clearly. The stories were to encourage fortitude under persecution and attack, while the revelations were to confirm that whatever Antiochus was doing at that moment, God's purposes were being worked out in the long term and were unalterable. But having said this one has not explained everything. On what materials did the author depend? What were the spiritual and intellectual ancestries of the book? Opinions on the latter of these two questions are divided and I will cite three examples from around the year 1960 as typical of three schools of thought. First, Martin Rist in the *Interpreter's Dictionary of the Bible* (1962) defined 'Apocalypticism' as 'a type of religious thought which apparently originated in Zoroastrianism, the ancient Persian religion; taken over by Judaism in the exilic and postexilic periods, and mediated by Judaism to Christianity.' Three years earlier, in 1959, Otto Plöger in his *Theokratie und Eschatologie* put the emphasis very differently: 'The connection between prophecy and apocalyptic has never been seriously disputed, and there is also widespread agreement that this connection finds embodiment in a common eschatological outlook.'[1] Such statements of agreement in the scholarly world are always risky, and the very next year, 1960, Gerhard von Rad in the second volume of his *Die Theologie des Alten Testaments* dissented, as follows: 'In view of its keen interest in the last things and of the significance it attaches to visions and dreams, it might seem appropriate to understand apocalyptic literature as a child of prophecy. To my mind, however, this is completely out of the question. . . . The decisive factor, as I see it, is the incompatibility between apocalyptic literature's view of history and that of the prophets.'[2] Later he offers his further opinion that 'the real matrix from which apocalyptic literature originates' is 'Wisdom' and refers to it as an attempt to understand the laws of the universe, which developed into an 'encyclopaedic science' covering history as well.[3]

The contradictions between the three views are less than these quotations might suggest if one studies the whole presentation of each writer, and it is not my intention to pursue this matter at length. Instead I propose to state my own position briefly in relation to them, and then to proceed to my first question about the materials used, since it is there that real progress can be reported.

I opt most nearly for Plöger's view. I find Rist's lacking proof, and von Rad's seems to me more posturing than a careful balancing of the relevant factors. Rist, you will remember, prefixed his whole definition with 'apparently', which is needed in view of the difficulty of ascertaining exactly what Zarathushtra taught. There is a long tradition behind the extant writings and only very confused material spread in the Hellenistic world. Dualism is the touchstone of this case, but if one only means that there is good and evil at work in the world, and that in a future conflict between the two good will prevail, then the prophets from Amos to Malachi so taught, even if we cannot be sure that Amos' understanding of the matter was exactly the same as Malachi's. The more international presentation of these concepts in apocalyptic as compared with prophecy reflects of course the change in historical circumstances, and the prophets could be equally international when they chose. Amos himself, after asking whether Yahweh had not brought Israel out of Egypt, added 'and the Philistines from Caphtor and the Syrians from Kir'?[4] Whether minor matters such as the angelology of apocalyptic could have been influenced by Zoroastrianism cannot be decided with certainty for the present, and the matter is not of fundamental importance when the continuity of basic ideas from prophecy to apocalyptic is so obvious and the cultural continuity not in dispute. Von Rad's rejection of this point overlooks, as it seems to me, the passage of time, the changed circumstances and the difference in medium. We are not of course minimizing the differences, nor denying that a Wisdom tradition could also be involved—pre-exilic prophets after all quote proverbs—but to us the differences seem superficial rather than fundamental, as to von Rad. He misses in apocalpytic the exhortatory material mingled in prophetic eschatology. Amos warned Israel and Jeremiah Judah that because of their sins they would be carried into captivity by the Assyrians and Babylonians respectively. And so they were. But there was no Hebrew prophet when Alexander's empire rose with such dramatic speed and then disintegrated equally rapidly. Furthermore, the Jews were virtually untouched by it. So we should not be too surprised that the author of Daniel concentrates on world empires and does not draw from them moral lessons for Israel beyond that 'the Most High rules in the kingdom of men'.[5] As to medium, the prophets were normally preachers whose message was intended to guide the whole Israelite community. Thus they covered all aspects of life and belief. The writers of apocalyptic were not oral preachers, but authors of specialised works, often intended, it seems, for a limited circle of readers, rather than as preaching material for the masses. It is hardly right to deny their dependence on the prophetic tradition because they concentrated on one aspect of prophetic teaching.

Daniel does of course declare his dependence on Jeremiah, and here the starting point was the seventy-year captivity prophesied by Jeremiah.[6] But whence the technique of interpreting this as seventy weeks of years? Was this done for the first time in Daniel, or was it something absorbed from the environment? We are now in to our first question about the materials used in the writing of the book. The difficulties here arise from the extreme paucity of Jewish writings from the century or two before Daniel. It is tempting to compare foreign material, like Zoroastrianism, with all the uncertainties that that involves. A reading of Deutero-Isaiah's denunciations of Babylonian gods, and of Ezra's handling of the mixed marriages might suggest that the shutters had been pulled down and no foreign influences could infiltrate into this exclusive community. But, at the same time that the prophet was preaching, his people were quietly forgetting their own month names and henceforth, even after the return, they used Babylonian month names instead. And the Chronicler, whose work continues with the record of Ezra's activities, had no compunction in assessing the contributions from the heads of families and military officers to the cost of building Solomon's temple in Persian darics. There is nothing here of the spirit of the French Academy which tried to keep Gallic speech free from such Anglicisms as 'toast' and 'week end'. The Israelites had often assimilated matter from other nations, though turning it to their own uses. Hebrew poetry borrowed a large amount of phraseology and imagery from Canaanite poetry, and Solomon's temple was in design and workmanship Phoenician, though this does not of course prove that Hebrew and Phoenician religion were the same.

A well known example of a foreign parallel to predictive prophecy occurs in an inscription of Esarhaddon, king of Assyria. Just as Jeremiah predicted a seventy-year captivity, so Marduk, god of Babylon, predicted a seventy-year desolation of his city when Sennacherib destroyed it. The god Marduk relented however, and, changing the position of the two sexagesimal digits used to write 70, made it 11, so that in Esarhaddon's reign the city was rebuilt.[7] All this happened before Jeremiah's birth. While it is not impossible that Jeremiah somehow heard of these happenings, it is much less likely that the author of Daniel could have done so, but it is the reinterpretation of the figure in each case which gives most point to this parallel. By itself, then, this case supplies more fascination than illumination.

Two more substantial matters where the form of Daniel is not derived from Hebrew prophecy merit serious consideration: first, the concept of world history as consisting of four succeeding empires, and secondly the technique of presenting history in concise annalistic form with names omitted and with verbs in the future tense.

First, the four world empires. This idea is presented twice in Daniel, in Nebuchadnezzar's vision in ch. 2, and in the succession of four animals arising from the sea in ch. 7. Nebuchadnezzar saw in vision an image made of different metals: head of gold, breast and arms of silver, belly and thighs of copper, the legs of iron, the feet part iron and part clay. The head is interpreted for us as Nebuchadnezzar himself, and the other metals represent succeeding kingdoms, which are not identified in the book. Until comparatively recently it appeared that the Book of Daniel was the source of all such schemes of world history, but an article by J. W. Swain in *Classical Philology* for 1940 brought decisive evidence of a much wider and earlier circulation of such schemes than was previously known. David Flusser's article in *Israel Oriental Studies* 2 (1972) 148–75 conveniently summarises all the material with the exception of traditional Hindu and Buddhist texts[8] so that I need offer a short summary only.

There are three elements in play: first, the idea of four world ages represented by different metals; secondly, the concept of four world empires; and thirdly, an associated group of ten, whether it be ten kings, world rulers, centuries, generations, weeks, or jubilees. (The ten come in Daniel as the ten horns on the last animal to rise from the sea.) The four metallic ages appear first in Hesiod's *Works and Days* lines 109ff, a Greek poem hardly later than the 7th century and perhaps earlier, but in any case before the Neo-Babylonian empire. Here the golden age of human bliss is followed by an inferior silver age, then by a copper age still more inferior. The fourth age marks an improvement and has no metallic association, so seeming out of place. So the fifth arrives, the present age of iron, characterised by all kinds of social unrest. Four metal ages occur in Zoroastrian texts. There are three passages in Pahlavi literature, which may date in their present form to only the sixth century A.D., but are considered to be based on a lost Avestan document. According to this late tradition Ahuramazda granted Zarathushtra a vision of a tree with four branches, one of gold, one of silver, a third of steel, and the fourth of 'mixed iron'. They are interpreted as four ages spanning the whole of human history. A variant form of this tradition offers seven branches representing seven periods, the metals being gold, silver, brass, copper, lead, steel and 'mixed iron'.

The scheme of four world empires originated in Persia, but only developed in Hellenistic times. The Persians were unknown in the Near East before the beginning of the first millennium B.C., when they immigrated into the area. As they settled down the Assyrians were a world power, which impinged on the newcomers. So to the Persians the Assyrians were the first world empire. Hence the origin of Ninus, that mythical first or second king of Assyria, who plagued classical antiquity and the European world until the decipherment of cuneiform. In due time the Assyrians were overthrown by the joint efforts of Medes and Babylonians, but to the Persians it appeared that their neighbours the Medes were responsible, so they became the second world empire in the Persian view of history. Before long the Persians overthrew both Medes and Babylonians to become the third world empire, and in overthrowing the Persians in turn Alexander founded the fourth empire. The earlier stages of this scheme are known from the Greek Herodotus and Ktesias, who drew on Persian sources for the succession: Assyrians, Medes, Persians, and the final form was taken over by Roman writers starting in the first half of the second century B.C.

The associated 'ten' is alluded to in the Zoroastrian source, where the last of the ten is synchronised with the running out of the last of the four world ages. It occurs also in Sibylline oracles, the Book of Enoch, a Dead Sea Scroll and later Jewish writings.

In my opinion only one solid conclusion results: that the Book of Daniel is employing traditional motifs in its presentation of the four world kingdoms. Flusser would like to go further. With advice of Shaul Shaked he inclined to assume an ultimate Persian source or sources for both Hesiod and Daniel.[9] Mary Boyce in contrast considers it possible that the Zoroastrian material was absorbed from foreign, that is Hellenistic sources,[10] and the possibility of such influence in general in the formation of the Avestan canon cannot be denied. The 'ten' motif occurs in Daniel and Pahlavi, but not in Hesiod. So long as the dating of the Zoroastrian evidence remains uncertain it will be impossible to draw any valid conclusion on the priority of Daniel or the Avestan tradition. The nearest thing to certainty in this matter is that the three sources attesting metal ages or kingdoms, Hesiod, Daniel and the lost Avesta, are not directly dependent on each other, so that lost sources, written, oral or both, must be presumed. Daniel therefore depended on one or more of these.

The concise annalistic history occurs of course in ch. 11, for example:

> A mighty king shall arise who will rule a great empire and do as he pleases. When he has arisen his kingdom shall be shattered and divided according to the points of the compass . . . (11: 3–4a)

which alludes of course to Alexander the Great. This style is more remarkable than has generally been acknowledged, since it is the only portion of prophetic or apocalyptic writing that has served as a source for historians Jewish, Christian and pagan from antiquity to modern times. To our knowledge the prophets never gave such detailed history. There was, however, a tradition of this in ancient Mesopotamia. Cuneiform tablets have yielded quite a number of texts which offer historical events in the form of *vaticinia ex eventu*. They do not all seem to be of one kind, but there are now three examples offering concise annalistic history with names censored and verbs in the future tense, two of which have been published only very recently. The first appeared in 1923[11] and is a piece of a Late Assyrian tablet from Assur, not later than 614 B.C. then, and not likely to be more than a century older, though the text could of course be older than the surviving copy. I quote a few lines:

> A prince will arise and will exercise kingship for 13 years. There will be an attack of Elam on Babylonia and the booty of Babylonia will be carried off. The shrines of the great gods will be ruined and Babylonia will be defeated. There will be chaos, upset and trouble in the land, and the upper classes will lose power. Some other, unknown person will arise, will seize power as if a king, and will kill off the nobility.[12]

This occurs in a group of sections all of which begin 'a prince will arise and rule for . . . years', and it is most probable that, despite a difference between one length of reign here and the figure in the only surviving king list for this period, the kings of Babylon Melišipak, Merodach-baladan I, Zababa-šuma-iddina and Enlil-nādin-aḫi are meant.[13] They ruled during the first half of the twelfth century B.C. and it is only our almost total ignorance about the events of their reigns that prevents us from being sure that these are the ones meant.[14]

The second text of this kind was excavated at Warka, Babylonian Uruk, Biblical Erech, in 1969. The tablet was apparently part of a private library belonging to an incantation priest Anu-ikṣur or another member of his family, and it was probably written during the Seleucid period, though again the text may have been composed at an earlier date. I quote an extract:

> After him a king will arise and will not judge the judgment of the land, will not give decisions for the land, but he will rule the four world regions and at his name the regions will tremble. After him a king will arise from Uruk and will judge the judgment of the land, will give decisions for the land. He will confirm the rites of Anu in Uruk . . . (rev. 9–12)

H. Hunger published the reverse (most of the obverse is broken off) in the preliminary excavation report in 1972,[15] and the whole thing in his volume *Spätbabylonische Texte aus Uruk*, Teil I (1976), as No. 3, in each case with translation. He joined with S. A. Kaufman to give a slightly different translation and an interpretation in

Journal of the American Oriental Society 95 (1975) 371ff, and another attempt at interpretation on the basis of the preliminary excavation report was offered by P. Höffken in *Die Welt des Orients* 9 (1977) 57ff. The latter offers no precise explanation of the whole content, but concludes from the historical allusions considered generally that it must have been composed between 700 and 538 B.C. Hunger and Kaufman use the references to the removal and return of the '(female) protecting spirit' as the key, and, assuming that this refers to the statue of the chief goddess of Uruk, Ishtar (by no means a certain assumption), they identify the king who removed it as Erība-Marduk, king of Babylon in the middle of the 8th century B.C., and the king who returned it as Nebuchadnezzar II. The evidence for this matter is a trifle inconsistent. Nebuchadnezzar himself refers to his returning both a male and a female statue to Uruk, but it is not clear that they were those of the chief male and female deities of the city. The later Nabonidus in his usual antiquarian interest tells how the goddess Ishtar of Uruk (i.e. her statue) was removed by the citizens of Uruk to Babylon under the reign of Erība-Marduk and was returned by a king whose name is broken off. From the context it could have been either Nabopolassar or Nebuchadnezzar II. One might overlook these difficulties if the resulting interpretation made sense of the whole text, but it does not. No proposals are made for most of the kings alluded to, and the text is made to end with Evil-Merodach described as ruling 'like a god', though in fact he lasted two years only and was uniformly condemned in the ancient world as a bad king. My own proposal is based on the succession of rulers. The first preserved one came from the Sea Land, that is by the Persian Gulf, and ruled from Babylon. He was followed by four kings, all of whom, as already quoted, did not rule the land and so receive no approbation. Two good kings, father and son, originating from Uruk, end the list. I take the Sea-Lander as Merodach-baladan II, well known from his embassy to Hezekiah, and he belonged to the Bit-Yakin tribe which did in fact occupy territory in the Sea Land. Then the four bad kings who shirked their duties are the Assyrians Sargon II, Sennacherib, Esarhaddon and Ashurbanipal, and the two good kings are Nabopolassar and his son Nebuchadnezzar, the founders of the Neo-Babylonian empire.[16] The document is clearly a product of the city of Uruk, which had very ancient cultural traditions that had been maintained, but was not the political capital, that position being indisputably Babylon's. Thus the Urukean prophecy has tacitly passed over all the Assyrian puppet rulers in Babylon and records only their Assyrian masters: a combination of chauvinism and political realism. It is not possible to demonstrate from other evidence that all the things said about this sequence of seven kings did in fact happen. We are far from well informed about the details of this period, especially as they were seen from Uruk, but equally nothing said can be shown to be wrong.[17] On these grounds this document must have been composed in Uruk after Nebuchadnezzar's accession in 605 B.C.

The third text is written on a much broken Late Babylonian tablet which reached the British Museum in 1881, but was overlooked until identified by A. K. Grayson recently. It is published in his book *Babylonian Historical-Literary Texts* (1975) with translation and explanation. Parts of two columns of writing remain on each side, but there is not one complete line, and only few can be restored. I give a sample:

> A rebel prince will arise [. . .] the dynasty of Harran [. . .] for 17 years [he will exercise kingship] and will prevail over the land. The festival of Esagil(?) [. . .] the wall in Babylon [. . .] he will plot evil against Babylonia. A king of Elam will rise up, the sceptre [. . .] he will remove him from his throne [. . .] he will seize the throne . . . (op. cit., p. 33 lines 11ff)

This refers of course to Nabonidus, who reigned for 17 years and was deposed by Cyrus, called here 'king of Elam'. Grayson has soberly worked out the historical details of the surviving text. The first column deals with the rise of the Neo-Babylonian empire, probably under Nabopolassar, though Nebuchadnezzar II might be meant. The second column deals with Neriglissar, Nabonidus and Cyrus. The third column takes up Arses and Darius III, referring to the eunuch Bagoas, then comes Alexander of Macedon, who is strangely said to have been defeated by Darius III with Babylonian help after inflicting an initial defeat on the Persian. The very badly preserved last column dealt with one more reign for certain, and perhaps with two others also, not to mention what might have been in the gap between the last two columns.

Columns on cuneiform tablets run from left to right on the obverse and from right to left on the reverse, and tablets are turned from top to bottom, not from side to side like our pages. As edited this text passes directly from Cyrus at the bottom of column II to Arses at the top of column III, which is most peculiar. Where is Darius I, Xerxes and the rest? The solution is that the tablet originally had three columns each side, not two as postulated in the *editio princeps*, and the completely missing columns III and IV covered these missing kings. What survive therefore are columns I and II, and V and VI.

Thus this document gave, in the form of predictions, a history of kings of Babylon from the rise of the Neo-Babylonian empire to the Hellenistic age. The main historical problem is the unhistorical defeat of Alexander by Darius III after which Babylonia enjoys peace and prosperity. If the text ended at that point one would say that it was composed after Alexander's first defeat of the Persians at Granicus to encourage the Babylonians to help Darius against the invader. However, the text continues with more reigns, though too broken to specify.

The striking similarity of these three Babylonian texts to Daniel 11 needs no underlining and poses the question of a possible connection. The Babylonian genre certainly antedates the rise of Jewish apocalyptic, and it was still being produced in the Hellenistic age. We do not in fact know who is supposed to be making these predictions in the cuneiform texts, since in two cases the beginnings are completely missing, and in the other case it is too badly damaged to be informative. But in reality this is not such a great loss since Daniel is a Jewish work and if it depended in this case on a cuneiform genre, it has used it within the traditions of Hebrew prophecy. There is of course no simple answer to this question. It is a matter of weighing relevant factors to decide whether it is probable that the author of Daniel or an antecedent author became acquainted with something of the Babylonian genre and was stimulated to create a Jewish counterpart. What has been learnt about the scheme of four world empires encourages us to make the inquiry.

Jews in Palestine, as well as those in Babylonia in the Hellenistic period, would certainly know of the existence of Babylonian learning, but in general the formidable cuneiform script would prevent any first-hand acquaintance. However, once this barrier had been overcome there was much to interest Jewish scholars since in the matter of the creation and earliest history of mankind Jewish and Babylonian traditions were related, and Babylonian history impinged on Israelite history during the later monarchy, the exile, and thereafter. The Babylonian scholar Berossus, by putting this and other material into Greek in the first half of the third century B.C., provided access, and Josephus was not the first Jew to exploit it. Eupolemus, one of the Maccabean envoys to Rome, shows dependence in his statement that Babylon was the first city to be settled after the flood,[18] since this occurs in Berossus, but not in the Bible. Most modern scholars have assigned this fragment to an unknown Samaritan author because it located Melchizedek's shrine on mount Gerizim, but without reason in my opinion. Salem, Melchizedek's town in Genesis 14, occurs again in Genesis 33:18 as understood by the LXX and the Book of Jubilees among others, where it is described as 'a city of Shechem'. Gerizim is a reputable place in the Hebrew Pentateuchal traditions, and it is not certain that the Samaritans substituted Gerizim for Ebal in their recension of Deuteronomy 27:4. The Old Latin version, which in other places attests the earliest attainable Hebrew reading, here agrees with the Samaritan text in reading Gerizim. It is now accepted that caution is needed before ascribing anti-Samaritan bias to Judaean Jews of the second century B.C., and in this light one can accept that a historian like Eupolemus may well have preferred the evidence of Genesis on this matter to that of the temple hymnbook (I refer to Psalm 76).[19]

Eupolemus' story, in an undisputed fragment,[20] that the Median Astibares accompanied Nebuchadnezzar on his campaign against Jerusalem is no doubt unhistorical and so not from Berossus, but is probably influenced by Ktesias, who also names a Median king Astibares.[21] But this still illustrates the desire to use non-Biblical sources. From Alexander Polyhistor in the first century B.C. and from other sources we know of the compilation of world chronicles from everything available, Greek, Jewish, Phoenician, Egyptian and Babylonian. For example, Abraham was synchronised with Babylonian or Assyrian kings, and Titan and Prometheus were synchronised with the Tower of Babel. Some of this production was certainly Jewish work.[22] Further evidence of Jewish interest in Babylonian writings comes from the existence of a Hebraised version of Berossus. As now read the text of the myth of origins contains doublets. One, following genuine Babylonian tradition, begins from water alone, The other version has both water and darkness as primaeval elements.[23] I assume that the latter was borrowed from Genesis, and before the time of Alexander Polyhistor. The opening of his Hebraised version survives, so far unnoticed, in Syriac.[24]

So far we have only a tentative circumstantial case: ch. 11 of Daniel is very similar in style and content to a Babylonian genre which was still productive in Hellenistic times, and Jewish interest in such things did exist at the time. But the case can be much strengthened. First, the lack of comparable material elsewhere is worth noting. The nearest things from Egypt, the so-called Demotic Chronicle and similar material in the just-published Archive of Ḥor,[25] though dating from roughly the middle of the second century A.D., is entirely different in style and partly different in content. It consists of obscure oracular utterances which are explained, some as prophesies of historical events. In Greek I have not discovered any fully comparable texts antedating Daniel. It remains, then, to show that this Babylonian genre could have been disseminated in a form intelligible to Jews. Either Greek or Aramaic could have been used. The former only came into use in Babylon with Alexander of Macedon, but Aramaic had been the ordinary language of the place for some centuries back. There is evidence that Babylonian material spread in the Hellenistic world in Aramaic, though little can be expected when Aramaic was normally written on leather and other perishable materials. Bowman in *Journal of Near Eastern Studies* 3 (1944) 219ff published extracts from a papyrus, presumably from Egypt, written in Aramaic, but in Demotic script. Though not a Babylonian document, it contains four lines of religious content (the last four of the six-line quotation on p. 227) that could easily have been translated verbatim from Babylonian. It strongly contrasts with the mishmash of spurious items about Babylon that are characteristic of Greek Hellenistic literature.[26] Babylonian Wisdom literature also influenced its Aramaic counterpart. The Elephantine Ahiqar has least to offer in this connection, but the other collection of sayings under his name, found in Syriac, Arabic, etc., shows clear Babylonian or Assyrian influence. The Babylonians of the Hellenistic age were proud to acknowledge this man. A tablet from Uruk copied out on 14th July 165 B.C. records 'Aba-Ninnu-dari, the scholar, in the time of Esarhaddon, whom the Arameans call Aḫuqar, [in Greek?] he is Niqaqru'.[27] Babylonian omens are also thought to lie behind some Egyptian omens of the Roman period, Greek astrological texts, and possibly Arabic omens.[28] It is a fact that the very best Babylonian mathematical astronomy was communicated to the Greeks in Hellenistic times, when, in the whole world, only the Babylonians had detailed records of astronomical phenomena going back for some centuries, and highly sophisticated mathematical systems for extrapolating from them. While there is no reason to suppose that any Greek learnt to read and use the appropriate cuneiform tablets, their debt was made plain in antiquity and is acknowledged today. Presumably learned Babylonians took the pains to teach Greeks in Greek. This of course was highly specialized—Berossus himself knew nothing of it—but if one asks what other product of Babylonian civilization might have been so popular as to merit translation into Aramaic or Greek, then prophecies are an obvious possibility. The Hellenistic age was the age of the proliferation of Sibyls, the multiplication of oracles, the birth of the horoscope, and much else of the same kind.

In such a syncretistic age as the Hellenistic it is certainly possible, perhaps even probable, that the author of Daniel adapted the style of a traditional Babylonian genre for his own purposes. It may be noted that other Jewish and Christian apocalyptic writings, though not Daniel, follow the convention of the Babylonian predictions in using names of previous peoples as pseudonyms for contemporary powers. Cyrus was said to be from Elam, not Persia, because Elam was the traditional Iranian neighbour of Babylon. The Macedonians were called Ḫanû, a troublesome nomadic group of the early second millennium. In the same way Edom is used for Rome in Jewish writings, and Babylon for the supreme enemy in the New Testament Apocalypse.

Study of background means studying the bricks not the building. Lest we should fail to see the wood for the trees, I must in conclusion stress that in drawing attention to the materials and models used in Daniel I am not wishing to detract from the importance of the finished work. Its author was in line of descent from the Hebrew prophets and wrote when his nation and its faith was in danger. How different world history might have been if the spirit of resistance had not existed in this man and his contemporaries. Had Antiochus IV succeeded, Judaism might have withered among sectarian groups in the Diaspora. Christianity might never have been born. Then there would have been no Bible, and no Ethel M. Wood lectures.

NOTES

1. P. 38, from English translation by S. Rudman, *Theocracy and Eschatology*, p. 27.

2. Vol. II, pp. 315–16, from English translation by D. M. G. Stalker, *Old Testament Theology*, vol. II p. 303.

3. Op. cit., II p. 319, English translation, p. 306.

4. 9:7.

5. 4:17, 25, 32.

6. Jer. 25:12, cf. Dan. 9:2.

7. R. Borger, *Die Inschriften Asarhaddons Königs von Assyrien* (*Archiv für Orientforschung*, Beiheft 9), p. 15, Episode 10a.

8. See e.g. J. Hastings, *Encyclopaedia of Religion and Ethics*, arts. 'Ages of the World (Buddhist)' and 'Ages of the World (Indian)'. The difficulties of fixing this material chronologically are so great that its value for the present interest cannot be assessed.

9. Tentatively on p. 167 of his article cited above, more emphatically on p. 173.

10. *A History of Zoroastrianism* (*Handbuch der Orientalistik*, ed. B. Spuler, I. Abteilung, 8. Band, I. Abschnitt, Lief. 2, Heft 2A) I p. 288.

11. E. Ebeling, *Keilschrifttexte aus Assur religiösen Inhalts* II no. 421.

12. Loc cit., ii 9–15, cf. A. K. Grayson and W. G. Lambert, *Journal of Cuneiform Studies* 18 (1964), pp. 12–16.

13. This was first proposed by E. Weidner, *Archiv für Orientforschung* 13 (1939/40), p. 236 and remains very plausible. Hallo's suggestion to identify the four rulers in this sequence with four from the Second Isin dynasty is open to serious objections, see J. A. Brinkman, *A Political History of Post-Kassite Babylonia*, p. 129, n. 762.

14. These rulers are dealt with by J. A. Brinkman, *Materials and Studies for Kassite History*, I.

15. *26. und 27. vorläufiger Bericht über die von dem Deutschen Archäologischen Institut und der Deutschen Orient-Gesellschaft aus Mitteln der Deutschen Forschungsgemeinschaft unternommenen Ausgrabungen in Uruk-Warka*, p. 87.

16. Hunger and Kaufman were uncertain whether the five consecutive KI+MIN signs in line 8 'indicate that this king will commit the same things as his predecessor, or that five kings will follow who will do the same, or even that an unknown large number of kings will do the same.' On the assumption that these KI+MIN signs are used in the normal way, they must each refer to a word or phrase in sequence that can be recognized in the immediately preceding context. There seems to be one possibility only: (i) = *arkīšu*, (ii) = *šarru*, (iii) = *illâmma*, (iv) = *dīni māti ul idânu*,

(v) = *purussê māti ul iparras*: 'After him a king will arise and will not judge the judgment of the land, will not give decisions for the land.' Thus only one king is meant.

17. What is said of the Sea Land king has long been known of Merodach-baladan II. Oppression of Uruk by Sargon II as described for the first absentee king is not so far attested, but is perfectly possible. Sennacherib—ex hypothesi—has nothing in particular said about him, which could well reflect Urukean ambivalence at his sack of Babylon. While it was indeed sacrilege, Urukean chauvinism would hardly resent it. While King List A ascribes an eight-year reign to Sennacherib over Babylon, the so-called Canon of Ptolemy records this period as an interregnum. The former was correct *de facto*, the latter *de jure*, which proves that Sennacherib was not personally ruling in Babylon, otherwise he would have been present for the New Year rites and so have been king *de jure*. Esarhaddon's presumed carrying away of the plunder of Babylonia may simply reflect the local attitude to Assyrian taxation, while the ruling of the whole world ('the four quarters') by the last bad king and the second and last good king alone admirably fits the vast extent of the empires of Ashurbanipal and Nebuchadnezzar II. If the interpretation proposed is correct, Nabopolassar came from Uruk. The present writer has found no other account of his city of origin. The omission of Ashurbanipal's little known successors is no objection to the proposal made here: Berossus does the same.

18. See most recently B. Z. Wacholder, *Eupolemus, A Study of Judaeo-Greek Literature* on this subject generally, p. 313 for a translation of this fragment and p. 3 for comment and bibliography.

19. J. T. Milik, *The Books of Enoch*, p. 9, presents as a further reason for assigning this fragment to a Pseudo-Eupolemus 'the primordial role of Abraham as against that assigned to Moses in the Judaean tradition'. But Abraham's finding and dissemination of astrology need not have been derogatory to Moses' achievements. Since only the briefest Eupolemus excerpt deals with Moses (this is accepted by Wacholder as genuine, op. cit., pp. 71ff) caution should be observed. Were the whole context dealing with Moses surviving it might present a very different picture. And is there any proof that 2nd century B.C. Samaritans acknowledged this tradition of Abraham's achievements, and that it was considered heterodox in Jerusalem at that time?

20. See B. Z. Wacholder, op. cit., p. 312.

21. F. W. König, *Die Persika des Ktesias von Knidos* (*Archiv für Orientforschung*, Beiheft 18), p. 163, 1.

22. B. Z. Wacholder, op. cit., ch. 4 and literature there cited.

23. F. Jacoby, *Die Fragmente der griechischen Historiker*, III C, pp. 370–3.

24. In Jacob of Edessa, *Hexaemeron*, Book II (*CSCO*, *Scriptores Syri*, Series II, vol. 56, ed. I.-B. Chabot and A. Vaschalde (1928), p. 70, tr. A. Vaschalde (1932), p. 56). This excerpt is introduced as 'in the books of

the Chaldeans' and was drawn to the attention of the present writer by S. P. Brock as such. The present writer identified it as the lost beginning of the Hebraised Berossus.

25. W. Spiegelberg, *Die sogenannte Demotische Chronik*; J. H. Johnson, 'The Demotic Chronicle as an Historical Source', *Enchoria* 4 (1974), 1–17; J. D. Ray, *The Archive of Ḥor*, text 4.

26. Apart from isolated items, and few of those, the only substantial Hellenistic Greek sources that offer dependable Babylonian information are Berossus (and he was faked, see the writer in *Iraq* 38 (1976), 171–3, but genuine excerpts do survive) and the list of kings in the so-called Canon of Ptolemy, on which see J. A. Brinkman, *A Political History of Post-Kassite Babylonia*, pp. 22 and 323.

27. J. J. A. van Dijk apud, *XVIII. vorläufiger Bericht über die von dem Deutschen Archäologischen Institut und der Deutschen Orient-Gesellschaft aus Mitteln der Deutschen Forschungsgemeinschaft unternommenen Ausgrabungen in Uruk-Warka*, p. 45 lines 20–1, with the latter tentatively restored [*ia-man-i*]*š*.

28. For the Egyptian see R. A. Parker, *A Vienna Demotic Papyrus on Eclipse- and Lunar-Omina*, text A; for the Babylonian see C. Bezold and F. Boll, *Reflexe astrologischer Keilinschriften bei griechischen Schriftstellern* (Sitzungsberichte der Heidelberger Akademie der Wissenschaften, Phil.-hist. Klasse 1911/17); for the Arabic see T. Fahd, *Arabica*, 8 (1961), 30–58 and *La Divination Arabe*. So far it is not clear whether these omens, which have not been exactly identified in cuneiform, only by general style and content, reached the sources cited through Aramaic, Greek or both.